ON SAFARI

by Claire Watts
Illustrated by Louise Voce

Scholastic Canada Ltd.
123 Newkirk Road, Richmond Hill, Ontario, Canada L4C 3G5

In Africa there are lots of wild animals. Many of them live on the open plains. People take trips called safaris to watch the animals.

LIONS

Lions live together in groups known as prides. Two or three male lions, some lionesses and some cubs make up a pride.

Male lions have a hairy mane around their head and neck.

Lions spend most of the day sleeping. Some lions sleep in trees.

Lions eat a big meal every few days. The male lions always eat first, and the cubs eat last.

Lions from the same pride greet each other by rubbing cheeks.

ELEPHANTS

Elephants are the largest animals that live on land.

Elephants love water. They suck up water in their trunks and shower themselves.

Elephants use their tusks to strip bark from trees to eat. They also use them to defend themselves.

Elephants use their trunks like hands. They can pick up huge logs or tiny leaves quite easily.

Baby elephants suck their trunks, like babies suck their thumbs.

GIRAFFES

Giraffes are the tallest animals in the world.

Giraffes have small horns on their heads. These are covered in skin and look like small antlers.

When giraffes drink, they have to stretch their front legs wide so that they can reach the water.

Giraffes sleep during the hottest part of the day. Most giraffes sleep standing up, but some lie down.

Giraffes use their long necks to reach leaves high up in trees.

RHINOS

New-born rhinos do not have horns. Their horns start to grow when they are a few weeks old.

Rhinos use their strong horns to dig up trees so they can eat the roots.

Rhinos have very tough skin. They use their horns to defend themselves against attackers, but they usually run away instead of fighting.

Rhinos wallow in mud to keep themselves cool in the hot sun.

HIPPOS

Hippos have very heavy bodies. They move much more easily in water than on land.

Small birds keep a hippo clean. They pick insects off its skin, and out of its ears and nostrils.

Hippos often lie down in the water, with only their eyes, ears and nostrils showing above the water.

Hippos have huge teeth. They use their teeth to defend themselves.

Hippos can walk along on the bottom of a lake or river.

ZEBRAS

Zebras live in herds. They roam across the open plains eating grass and leaves.

Zebras use the tuft of hair at the end of their tail to get rid of flies.

Zebras have short, thick manes which stand up on their necks.

Zebras have wide black and white stripes. When zebras are gathered in a group, it is difficult to tell one from another.